Revised Edition

# Venus & Serena Williams

By Madeline Donaldson

AMAZING ATHLETES

 Lerner Publications Company/Minneapolis

Lerner Publications Company
A division of Lerner Publishing Group, Inc.
241 First Avenue North
Minneapolis, MN 55401 U.S.A.

Website address: www.lernerbooks.com

Library of Congress Cataloging-in-Publication Data

Donaldson, Madeline.
    Venus & Serena Williams / by Madeline Donaldson. — 2nd rev. ed.
        p.    cm. — (Amazing athletes)
    Includes bibliographical references and index.
    ISBN 978-0-7613-7463-3 (pbk. : alk. paper)
    1. Williams, Venus, 1980—Juvenile literature.  2. Williams, Serena, 1981—Juvenile literature.
    3. Tennis players—United States—Biography—Juvenile literature.  I. Title.  II. Title: Venus and
    Serena Williams.
    GV994.A1D65  2011
    796.3420922—dc22 [B]                                                        2010025780

Manufactured in the United States of America
1 — BP — 12/31/10

# TABLE OF CONTENTS

A big crowd came to see Venus and Serena play for the 2009 **Wimbledon** championship.

# GRAND SLAM SISTERS

Serena Williams looked across the court at her sister Venus and got ready to **serve**. Serena leaned back and tossed the ball in the air. Smack! The ball sailed past Venus before she could **return** it. Another **ace** for Serena!

Venus and Serena Williams are not only sisters. They are close friends. But on this day, they were **opponents**. The sisters were playing against each other in the **singles final match** at the 2009 Wimbledon tennis **tournament**.

Serena has one of the fastest serves in tennis.

Serena is focused on the tennis court.

Wimbledon is one of four **Grand Slam** tennis tournaments played every year. Venus had won the Wimbledon championship in 2007 and 2008. She would have to beat Serena if she wanted to win the tournament in 2009.

The first **set** was very close. Serena won in a **tiebreaker**. The second set was tied 2–2 when

Serena began to take control. She hit powerful returns and smashed huge serves. Venus tried to keep up with her younger sister. But Serena could not be stopped.

Women first played for the Wimbledon title in 1884. Maud Watson, 19, was the first female champion.

Venus leans out to return the ball.

The match ended when Venus hit a **backhand** into the net. Serena won in two sets, 7–6, 6–2. She sank to her knees on the court and raised her arms. Serena was Wimbledon champion!

Serena celebrates after Venus's final shot goes into the net.

Venus *(left)* and Serena *(right)* meet for a hug when the match is over.

Venus wanted to win, but she was happy for her sister. "She played the best tennis today, so congratulations," she said after the match.

The victory marked Serena's 11th Grand Slam championship. But this win at Wimbledon was special. She had not won the tournament since 2003. "Now that I won, I can say it," Serena said with a smile after her win. "It's really awesome."

Venus *(left)* and Serena *(right)* started playing tennis when they were very young. Their father, Richard, was their first coach.

# Growing Up

Venus and Serena Williams grew up in Compton, a town in Southern California. They were the youngest of five daughters. Their dad, Richard, had caught the tennis bug. He had been teaching their older sisters to play tennis.

In 1984, when Venus was four, she started hitting tennis balls with her family. A year later, when Serena turned four, she also picked up a racket for the first time. Before long, it was clear the two girls had a lot of natural talent. Their early skills amazed Richard and the girls' mother, Oracene. (Richard and Oracene divorced in 2003.)

Walls in the ghettos of Los Angeles often were covered with graffiti.

The Williamses' neighborhood was in the **ghetto**. This part of Compton had high crime rates. Gang violence was common. The neighborhood's tennis courts weren't in great shape. The Williams sisters had to be careful when they practiced. Sometimes fights broke out between the gangs near the courts and the girls would have to leave. But the danger didn't stop them from going to the courts nearly every day.

Richard wanted his daughters to be great tennis players. But he also wanted them to do well in school. He told Venus and Serena they couldn't play tennis if they hadn't done their homework. Both sisters worked hard at tennis and in school.

Over time, gang members came to respect what Richard and his daughters were doing on Compton's cracked courts. The gangs left them alone.

On Compton's courts, Richard pushes Venus in a ball-filled shopping cart.

Venus's tennis skills wowed a lot of coaches.

# TURNING PROFESSIONAL

Venus was the older sister by a little over a year. At aged nine, she began playing in and winning junior tennis tournaments. At the same time, Serena was also winning tournaments. They got a lot of attention when they played. The attention made it hard for them to focus on schoolwork. Richard decided Venus and Serena should stop playing junior tournaments.

The girls kept practicing, though. With their dad coaching them, they got better and better. They improved in both singles and **doubles** (when two two-person teams play). After many months, Richard felt he'd done what he could. His daughters needed a better coach.

Rick Macci, a tennis coach from Florida, flew to California. He couldn't believe how good the girls were. He called Venus a "female Michael Jordan." Coaching cost a lot of money. Rick offered to coach the girls for free. But the family would have to move to Florida. Venus and Serena's parents talked it over. They decided to quit their jobs and move the entire family to Florida.

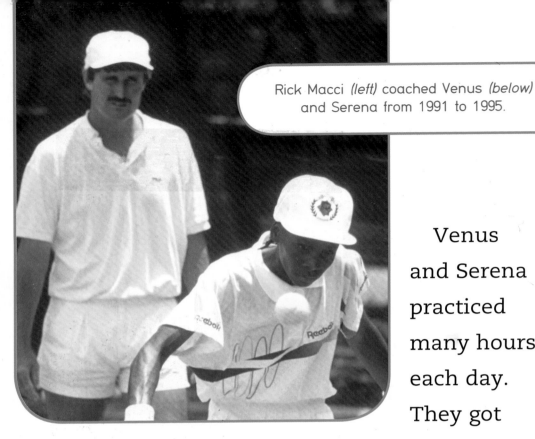

Rick Macci *(left)* coached Venus *(below)* and Serena from 1991 to 1995.

Venus and Serena practiced many hours each day. They got stronger. They gained more experience in singles and doubles. Instead of going to school, the girls were taught at home. Richard and Oracene were still very serious about education. They wanted their children to be smart people, not just smart tennis players.

In 1994, Venus started bugging her parents about turning **professional**. Even though she was only 14, Venus wanted her chance to play against the best women players. Her parents finally agreed. But she could only play in a certain number of tournaments a year. They put the same limits on Serena when she turned pro in 1995.

In October 1994, Venus played her first match as a professional. She won!

Companies approached the Williamses with offers of money if the girls would **endorse** (help sell) their products. The family signed contracts with companies that make sports equipment and clothing. The endorsement money helped pay for travel, housing, training partners, and other expenses.

Venus holds up tennis shoes made by Reebok. She first agreed to endorse Reebok products in 1995.

Serena *(between Richard and Venus)* is pretty quiet during an interview with reporters. Serena turned professional in 1995.

# LIFE AT THE TOP

After a few years playing pro tennis, the girls were ranked in the top 100 by the **Women's Tennis Association (WTA)**. In 1997, Venus made it to her first Grand Slam final at the **U.S. Open**. She lost to Martina Hingis.

Venus did not enjoy beating her sister at the 1998 Australian Open.

In 1998, the sisters played in the **Australian Open**. During the tournament, they had to play each other for the first time as professionals. Neither liked the experience much. "It wasn't funny, eliminating my little sister," Venus said after beating Serena.

Serena was the first Williams sister to win a Grand Slam singles event. In 1999, she beat

Hingis at the U.S. Open. Venus followed by winning Wimbledon in 2000. That same year, Venus and Serena took part in the Summer Olympic Games in Australia. They each took home a gold medal for their doubles play. Venus won a gold in singles.

Venus *(left)* and Serena *(right)* proudly show off their gold medals from the 2000 Olympics.

In 2001, the Williams sisters played each other for the first time in a Grand Slam final at the U.S. Open. Perhaps the pressure got to the sisters. Neither played her best tennis. Venus beat Serena in two sets.

By 2002, the sisters were used to playing each other in big tournaments. They reached the

The sisters hug each other after the 2002 French Open final. Serena won the match, 7–5, 6–3.

finals of the French Open, Wimbledon, and the U.S. Open that year. Serena won all three events.

Off the court, the Williams family suffered a terrible blow in September 2003. Yetunde Price, their older sister, was murdered in Compton. Then, in 2004, injuries plagued both tennis stars. But by 2005, the sisters were healthy and winning again. Venus won Wimbledon and Serena won the Australian Open that year.

Excited and happy, Venus holds up her 2005 Wimbledon trophy. She beat Lindsay Davenport in the final.

Venus *(left)* and Serena *(right)* attend a fashion show in New York City.

Meanwhile, the sisters showed fans their fashion talents. They began designing their own tennis outfits. Venus also started V Starr Interiors, her own interior design firm in Florida. Serena formed her own clothing line, Aneres.

Ongoing injuries kept both sisters off the court for most of 2006. As the Grand Slam events started in 2007, Venus and Serena showed their fans that they were back and better than ever.

Serena won the singles title at the Australian Open. Venus took the prize at Wimbledon.

In 2008, the sisters faced each other in the championship match at Wimbledon. Venus took the title for the fifth time. Venus and Serena were also playing well together. They won the doubles title at Wimbledon. The pair also competed for the United States in the 2008 Summer Olympics. They took home the gold medal for their doubles play.

Venus chats on the *Tonight Show with Conan O'Brien* in 2009. Venus and Serena have appeared on several talk shows.

Venus *(left)* and Serena *(right)* work together during the doubles competition at Wimbledon in 2009.

Serena began 2009 by winning the singles title at the Australian Open. She and Venus also took first place in doubles. After Serena beat Venus in the final match at Wimbledon in 2009, the two went on to win the doubles event. The duo later took home the doubles prize at the U.S. Open. For her many accomplishments in 2009, Serena was named the Associated Press Female Athlete of the Year.

Serena won the Australian Open for the fifth time in 2010. Later that year, she won her fourth Wimbledon singles title. With these two wins, she had thirteen Grand Slam singles titles. She passed the great Billie Jean King in the list. She and Venus won doubles titles at the Australian Open and the French Open.

Venus and Serena Williams have achieved amazing things in their tennis careers. In 2010, the WTA ranked Serena as the number one female tennis player in the world. Venus was ranked number two. "Serena and I, we both expect from ourselves great results," Venus says. "And maybe when all these moments are over, then we can look back and kind of be amazed."

Serena *(left)* and Venus *(right)* hold up their trophies after winning the 2009 Wimbledon doubles championship.

# Selected Career Highlights

## Venus's Career Highlights

**2010**    Won doubles titles at two Grand Slam events
(Australian Open and French Open)

**2009**    Won doubles titles at three Grand Slam events
(Australian Open, Wimbledon, and U.S. Open)

**2008**    Won her fifth Wimbledon singles title
Won doubles gold medal at the Summer Olympic
Games with Serena

**2007**    Won her fourth Wimbledon singles title
Withdrew from Australian Open with a wrist
injury

**2006**    Injuries limited her play throughout the year

**2005**    Won her third Wimbledon singles title

**2004**    Performed poorly at Grand Slam events, reaching the
quarterfinals only of the French Open

**2003**    Reached singles final of the Australian Open for the first time but
lost to Serena
Reached singles final of Wimbledon but lost to Serena
Reached singles final of the Australian Open for the first time

**2002**    Reached number one ranking for the first time

**2001**    Won singles titles at two Grand Slam events (Wimbledon and the
U.S. Open, when she beat Serena) and four other tour events

**2000**    Won singles titles at two Grand Slam events (Wimbledon and
the U.S. Open), and at three other tour events
Won the singles gold medal at the Olympic Games in Sydney,
Australia

**1999**    Won singles titles at six tour events

**1998**    Won singles titles at three tour events
Beat Serena in their first professional matchup in the opening
round of the Australian Open

**1997**    First woman since 1978 to reach the finals at her first
U.S. Open appearance

## Serena's Career Highlights

**2010** Won her fourth singles title at Wimbledon
Won her fifth singles title at the Australian Open
Won doubles titles at two Grand Slam events (Australian Open and French Open)

**2009** Won her fourth singles title at the Australian Open
Won her third singles title at Wimbledon
Won doubles titles at three Grand Slam events (Australian Open, Wimbledon, and U.S. Open)
Named Female Athlete of the Year by the Associated Press

**2008** Won her third singles title at the U.S. Open
Won doubles gold medal at the Summer Olympic Games with Venus

**2007** Won her third singles title at the Australian Open

**2006** Injuries forced her out of most tournaments, including Wimbledon and the French Open

**2005** Won her second singles title at the Australian Open

**2004** Injuries kept her off the court most of the year

**2003** Won singles title at the Australian Open for the first time
Successfully defended her 2002 Wimbledon singles title by defeating Venus
Along with Grand Slam wins from 2002, held titles in all four Grand Slam events, which was nicknamed a "Serena Slam"
Won singles title at the Australian Open for the first time
Along with Grand Slam wins from 2002, held titles in all four events

**2002** Won singles titles at three Grand Slam events (the French Open, Wimbledon, and the U.S. Open), all against Venus
Reached number one ranking for the first time (replacing Venus)
Named Female Athlete of the Year by the Associated Press

**2001** Won singles titles at two tour events

**2000** Won singles titles at three tour events

**1999** Won singles titles at one Grand Slam event (U.S. Open) and four other tour events

# Glossary

**ace:** a serve that a player is unable to return

**Australian Open:** the Australian Grand Slam event played every January. Players from around the world compete to win the Australian Open final in singles and doubles.

**backhand:** hitting the ball while holding the racket so that the back of the hand is facing the net

**doubles:** a tennis match in which two two-person teams play each other

**endorse:** to help sell products by appearing in ads on television or in magazines. The company that makes the products pays money to the person endorsing the products.

**final:** the last match in a series of tennis matches. The winner of the final match claims the championship for that year.

**ghetto:** a rundown area of a city

**Grand Slam:** in tennis, the name given to four championships played around the world each year. The events are the Australian Open, the French Open, Wimbledon (in England), and the U.S. Open.

**match:** a tennis contest that is won when one player or team wins a specified number of games and sets

**opponents:** the players on the other side, the challengers

**professional:** a status that allows an athlete to play in tournaments for money

**return:** the shot played by the player receiving the serve

**serve:** a hit of the tennis ball to start a tennis point

**set:** in a tennis match, a group of six or more games. A set must be won by at least two games or in a tiebreaker. Women's tennis matches have a maximum of three sets. The person who wins two of the sets wins the whole match. Winning two sets in a row is called winning in straight sets.

**singles:** a tennis match that pits one player against another

**tiebreaker:** a playoff to decide the winner of a set after both players have won six games. A player must win by at least two points more than the opponent.

**tournament:** a series of contests in which a number of people or teams take part, hoping to win the championship final

**U.S. Open:** the American Grand Slam event played every September in New York. Players from around the world compete to win the U.S. Open final in singles and doubles.

**Wimbledon:** the Grand Slam event played every June and July in Wimbledon, England. Players from around the world compete to win the Wimbledon final in singles and doubles.

**Women's Tennis Association (WTA):** the governing body of professional women's tennis players. The WTA determines tennis rankings. The rankings show how well a player is playing compared to other players.

# Further Reading & Websites

Bailey, Diane. *Venus and Serena Williams: Tennis Champions.* New York: Rosen Central, 2010.

Sandler, Michael. *Tennis: Victory for Venus Williams.* New York: Bearport Publishing, 2006.

Storey, Rita. *Tennis.* London: Franklin Watts, 2007.

Todd, Anne M. *Venus and Serena Williams: Athletes.* New York: Chelsea House Publications, 2009.

Vale, Mark. *Junior Tennis: A Complete Coaching Manual for the Young Tennis Player.* New York: Barrons Educational Series, 2006.


Sony Ericsson WTA Tour
http://www.sonyericssonwtatour.com/1/
The official website of the Sony Ericsson WTA Tour has rankings, late-breaking news stories, biographies, photographs, and more.

*Sports Illustrated Kids*
http://sikids.com/
The *Sports Illustrated Kids* website covers all sports, including tennis.

Venus and Serena Fan Website
http://www.venusandserena.homestead.com
This website provides fans with recent news stories, biographies, photographs, and more.

# Index

## Photo Acknowledgments

The images in this book are used with permission of: © Clive Brunskill/ Getty Images, pp. 4, 6, 23, 29; © Pool/Getty Images, p. 5; © Carl De Souza/ Pool/Getty Images, pp. 7, 8; © GLYN KIRK/AFP/Getty Images, p. 9; © Ken Levine/Getty Images, p. 10; © Joseph Sohm/Visions of America/CORBIS, p. 12; © Ken Levine /Allsport/Getty Images, pp. 13, 16; © Allsport UK / Allsport/Getty Images, p. 14; © Al Bello/Getty Images, p. 17; © Reuters/ CORBIS, p. 18; © Otto Greule Jr/Getty Images, p. 19; © WILLIAM WEST/AFP/ Getty Images, p. 20; © Gary M Prior/Allsport/Getty Images, p. 21; © FRANCOIS GUILLOT/AFP/Getty Images, p. 22; © Stephen Lovekin/Getty Images for IMG), p. 24; Margaret Norton/NBCU Photo Bank via AP Images, p. 25; AP Photo/Alastair Grant, p. 26; Press Association via AP Images, pp. 27, 28.

Cover: © Ryan Pierse/Getty Images (top); AP Photo/Rick Rycroft (bottom).